Original title:
Candlelight Frost

Copyright © 2024 Swan Charm
All rights reserved.

Author: Olivia Oja
ISBN HARDBACK: 978-9916-79-600-9
ISBN PAPERBACK: 978-9916-79-601-6
ISBN EBOOK: 978-9916-79-602-3

Whispering Embers in the Silent Snow

In the hush of night, soft flakes descend,
Embers glow bright, as shadows blend.
Whispers of warmth in the cold air,
Stories of fire, lost everywhere.

Through the stillness, memories dance,
Flickering hopes in a fleeting glance.
Each flake a tale, a gentle sigh,
Cradling dreams as the world drifts by.

Under the blanket, a quiet plea,
Time stands still, just you and me.
With every heartbeat, love ignites,
Even in darkness, we share our lights.

The night unfolds, a canvas bare,
Painting our moments, tender and rare.
Embers whisper secrets untold,
Wrapped in the warmth of the winter's fold.

As dawn approaches, the snow will gleam,
But in our hearts, we'll hold the dream.
Whispering embers in the silent glow,
Forever kindled beneath the snow.

Sweet Luminescence of the Falling Snow

Snowflakes dance in gentle flight,
Whispers soft, pure and bright.
Beneath the moon's tender gaze,
Winter's magic sets the blaze.

Blankets white upon the ground,
Silence deep, a tranquil sound.
Stars above twinkle and sigh,
As the world drifts, dreams fly high.

Crisp air filled with frosty cheer,
Nature's quilt is drawing near.
Heartbeats calm, wrapped so tight,
In the bliss of soft starlight.

Footprints trace a fleeting path,
Echoes caught in winter's wrath.
Yet in this sublime embrace,
Sweet luminescence finds its place.

Celestial Warmth in Frozen Repose

Midwinter's night, stars gleam and glow,
Wrapped in a blanket of soft white snow.
Underneath a silver sky,
Dreams of warmth and peace draw nigh.

A whispering breeze, so cool and light,
Carrying tales of day and night.
Frozen trees sway with grace,
Nature rests in a tranquil space.

Fires kindled in hearts aglow,
Against the chill, love's fervent flow.
Hands held close, a pulse so near,
Celestial warmth, forever dear.

Snowflakes fall like blessings sent,
In that stillness, hearts content.
The world glimmers in twilight's grace,
A frozen moment, a sacred space.

Whispered Light in a Frozen Twilight

Dusk descends with a tender hand,
Painting the sky in hues so grand.
Whispers swirl in icy air,
As twilight wraps the earth so fair.

Frosty breath and crystal dreams,
Nature's hush, or so it seems.
Soft light flickers, shadows play,
In a realm where night meets day.

Stars emerge, one by one,
In the chill, warmth has begun.
Holding closely hearth and hope,
In frozen realms, we learn to cope.

Each sparkling flake, a fleeting kiss,
Frozen twilight, a moment of bliss.
Together we weave, in silence bright,
Captured in the whispered light.

The Glow of Forgotten Seasons

Amidst the snow, lost tales unfold,
Whispers of warmth in the bitter cold.
Memories wrapped in frosty sheen,
The glow of seasons that once have been.

Eager hearts long for the sun,
Yet in winter's hold, we find our fun.
Echoes of laughter, soft and sweet,
In the chill, old friendships meet.

Each flake a story, each drift a sigh,
Underneath the vast, unyielding sky.
Time stands still as memories rise,
In the glow that softly lies.

Nature's palette, a frosty hue,
Revealing bright shades of joy anew.
In the silence, we take flight,
Chasing the glow of forgotten light.

Fiery Hues in Crystal Darkness

In shadows deep, the embers glow,
Whispers dance where cold winds flow.
Flickers of red and vibrant gold,
Stories of warmth in the night unfold.

Crimson rays on silvery frost,
Beauty found, though it is lost.
Each sparkle bright, a fading dream,
Silent echoes of a distant scream.

Through icy trails, the colors bleed,
Passion's light, a vital seed.
Glimmers of hope in the veiled dark,
Fiery hues that leave a mark.

Amidst the chill, the flames ignite,
Guiding hearts through the endless night.
With every flicker, shadows sway,
Fiery hues chase the bleak away.

Solace Found in Winter's Embrace

Snowflakes whisper on muted ground,
Softly falling, a peace profound.
Silent nights with starlit skies,
Winter's breath, a tender sigh.

Frosted trees in a crystal cage,
Nature rests, the seasons gauge.
In stillness deep, a heartbeat slow,
Time stands still beneath the snow.

Candles flicker, warm and bright,
Creating solace on the longest night.
Embraced by dark, we find our way,
In winter's hold, we softly stay.

Wrapped in silence, hearts combine,
Finding warmth in love's design.
The world outside may freeze and chill,
But in this space, our hearts are still.

Journey of Illuminated Solitude

A path unfolds with every step,
In quiet moments, secrets kept.
Wandering thoughts like stars at night,
Illuminated by inner light.

With every breath, the silence sings,
A melody of what solitude brings.
Footprints etched on a winding road,
Carried forward, away from the load.

Reflections dance in the mind's expanse,
Courage found in the stillness' glance.
Through empty fields, a spirit roams,
Each heartbeat echoes—this path is home.

In every pause, a truth revealed,
A quiet strength, a heart unsealed.
Journeying on, the soul takes flight,
Illuminated by its own soft light.

Light that Warms the Frozen Heart

In the depths of winter's grip,
Lies a longing, a gentle slip.
A flicker starts within the cold,
A story yearning to be told.

Through icy tendrils, love does creep,
Warming secrets that we keep.
A spark ignites, a gentle flame,
Dancing softly, calling your name.

Frozen hearts begin to thaw,
Touched by wonder, pulled by awe.
In tender moments, embers start,
To melt away the frozen heart.

Light that glows in darkest places,
Brings forth smiles, and tender faces.
As spring approaches, shadows part,
Breath of life, the warming heart.

A Veil of Warmth in Icebound Nights

In the silent shadows, warmth does weave,
A tapestry of dreams, what we believe.
Soft whispers echo through the frozen air,
Wrapped in comfort, we escape despair.

Stars gleam like diamonds in the starlit sky,
A canvas painted where our hopes can fly.
Each breath a cloud, drifting, blurring time,
Hearts beat to rhythms, a gentle chime.

The moon, a lantern, sparkles with delight,
Guiding us home through the coldest night.
With every heartbeat, the chill fades away,
In this sacred space, we choose to stay.

Embers glowing bright in the hearth's embrace,
Shadows dance lightly, a waltz of grace.
We gather our stories, shared under the glow,
In a veil of warmth, our spirits flow.

Timeless Glow of Winter's Memory

Frosted windows frame a world so still,
Time drips slowly, like a whispered thrill.
Remnants of snowflakes linger in the air,
Each moment cherished, a jewel so rare.

Footsteps crunch softly on powdered stone,
Reminders echo of paths we have known.
In swirling flurries, past laughter unfolds,
A timeless glow in the heart that holds.

Winter's breath kisses the frozen ground,
While echoes of joy in our minds abound.
Memories painted in hues of white and blue,
Each picture captured, a vivid view.

As daylight surrenders to twilight's embrace,
We're wrapped in warmth, our own secret space.
In the hush of the night, we find peace anew,
In winter's memory, we'll always be true.

Silken Hues Beneath the Chill

Underneath blankets of glistening snow,
Lives a soft warmth, a subtle glow.
Silken hues dance in the pale daylight,
Whispering softness, shadows take flight.

Petals once vibrant now frozen in time,
Yet their beauty lingers, a silent rhyme.
Touched by the frost, they shimmer and shine,
Nature's embrace, a delicate line.

The chill wraps around like an old, gentle friend,
Whispering tales of seasons that blend.
In the heart of winter, life's colors reside,
Waiting for moments when spring will abide.

With every sunset, the cold becomes bright,
Stars twinkle softly, guiding the night.
In silken hues, our dreams take their form,
Beneath the chill, our hearts stay warm.

Radiating Light in Frosty Rapture

In frosty nights where silence reigns supreme,
We find glowing embers of a warm dream.
A world adorned in glittering white frost,
In this rapture, we find what we thought lost.

Gentle whispers float through the snow-clad trees,
Carried on breezes that dance with ease.
Each moment shimmering, a radiant light,
Casting soft shadows in the depths of night.

Candles flicker, dreams begin to ignite,
Radiating warmth, defying the bite.
In the heart's embrace, the chill fades away,
In frosty rapture, we choose to stay.

Through veils of mist, the dawn starts to break,
Painting the world with hues we can make.
A reminder that light can pierce through the night,
In radiating warmth, we find our delight.

Celestial Brightness Amidst the Cold

Stars twinkle high in the night,
Amidst the chill, they bring light.
Whispers of warmth in the sky,
Guiding lost dreams as they fly.

Moonbeams dance on snowy hills,
Echoing silence, the heart stills.
In the depth of winter's fold,
Celestial stories unfold.

Each flake's descent, a silent shout,
In the dark, there's no doubt.
Beauty wrapped in icy sheen,
Lost in the realm of the unseen.

Winds cradle the midnight glow,
Carrying secrets only they know.
The chill that brushes the skin,
Is where my soul learns to begin.

Amidst the cold, warmth is found,
In connections that know no bound.
Celestial brightness leads the way,
In the heart of a winter's day.

Shimmering Hope in the Hush of Winter

Silent nights wrapped in white,
Where hopes shimmer with delight.
Snowflakes fall like dreams reborn,
Blanketing the world, a new morn.

Frigid air whispers sweet tales,
Of forgotten paths and hidden trails.
Beneath the frost, life still brews,
Waiting for the sun's warm hues.

Glistening thoughts dance in the air,
Winter's hush softens the despair.
In solitude's calm embrace,
Hope ignites in every space.

The world slows, a gentle sigh,
As starlit wishes drift high.
With each breath, the cold inspires,
A spark of warmth that never tires.

In the depth of winter's fold,
Shimmering hope, fiercely bold.
Amidst the stillness, dreams take flight,
Crafting joy from the frosted night.

Frosty Night's Gentle Embrace

In the stillness of the night,
Frosty kisses bring delight.
Whispers weave through icy trees,
Carried softly on the breeze.

Moonlight bathes the earth in glow,
Lighting paths where shadows flow.
A blanket of peace wraps tight,
In the warmth of winter's light.

Stars peek through the endless dark,
Holding close a comforting spark.
Each breath fogs in the cold air,
Creating magic everywhere.

Crystalline beauty transforms the scene,
In night's embrace, acting serene.
Soft sighs of nature, pure and bright,
Frosty night holds dreams in flight.

As sleep falls 'neath this quilted sky,
I've learned to breathe, to wonder why.
In winter's arms, I find my place,
Embraced tenderly by time and space.

Frosted Glow of Dusk's Palette

Evening sighs, the day takes flight,
A frosted glow, a soft twilight.
Colors blend in a gentle sweep,
As the world falls into sleep.

Icicles hang, a crystal show,
Painting the landscape in frosted glow.
Every hue tells a story old,
Of warmth wrapped in winter's cold.

Soft whispers of the coming night,
Bring forth dreams, a soothing sight.
Nature's canvas, brushed with care,
A magic moment, light as air.

As dusk deepens, shadows play,
Encircling the earth in gray.
Still, there's beauty in the chill,
Frosted reflections that time will fill.

Embrace the wonders brought by fate,
In the stillness, we contemplate.
A palette rich, a heart that knows,
In winter's arms, beauty grows.

Radiance amid a Chill

The frost clings close to every tree,
But warmth seeps through, a memory.
In shadows deep, a light does gleam,
Whispers of hope in the cold's regime.

Soft glows emerge from hidden spaces,
Embracing the night with tender graces.
Each flicker speaks of journeys bright,
In the heart's hearth, a fire ignites.

Snowflakes dance like fleeting dreams,
Caught in the glow of silver beams.
Radiant moments, we hold them tight,
As warmth entwines the lingering night.

Through winter's chills, our spirits rise,
A gentle warmth beneath the skies.
In the silence, love's path we find,
A radiant bond that time designed.

Twilight's Gentle Caress

As day fades into a soft embrace,
Twilight weaves magic, a serene trace.
Colors blend in the evening's sigh,
A canvas crafted in the fading sky.

Breezes whisper through the swaying grass,
Moments linger, as shadows pass.
The hush of twilight cradles the world,
Secrets revealed as daylight unfurled.

Stars emerge, a gentle light,
Guiding dreams into the night.
In twilight's arms, we find our peace,
A tender pause, a sweet release.

The horizon blushes, a lover's kiss,
In the twilight's glow, we find our bliss.
Every heartbeat syncs with the dusk,
A quiet promise, an ancient trust.

A Glow Against the Dark

In shadows deep, a spark ignites,
A gentle glow breaks through the nights.
Against the dark, its warmth does stand,
A beacon bright in a silent land.

Each flicker tells of strength and grace,
Illuminating the quiet space.
Hope dances in the softest light,
A brave companion through the night.

The heartbeat echoes, steady, clear,
In every pulse, we conquer fear.
A glow against the vast unknown,
Together, never stands alone.

From deep within, our stories spark,
Each tale a glow against the dark.
In unity, our spirit shines,
A luminous path, our fate aligns.

Euphoria in Vanilla Haze

The air is sweet with a fragrant kiss,
In every breath, a fleeting bliss.
Vanilla swirls in a dreamy haze,
Wrapped in warmth of sunny days.

A melody flows like a soft refrain,
In each warm note, there's no more pain.
Joy blossoms in the heart's embrace,
In euphoria, we find our place.

With laughter shared, our spirits soar,
In this gentle haze, we crave for more.
Moments linger, tender and light,
In the vanilla glow of paradise.

Whispers of joy weave through the air,
Every heartbeat, a love laid bare.
In sweetness, we'll forever stay,
Euphoria holds us, come what may.

Mystic Glimmers of Chilling Twilight

Whispers shadow the fading light,
Stars awaken from their flight.
Glimmers dance on frosty air,
Cascades of dreams, beyond compare.

Moonbeams weave a tale so grand,
Twilight's brush paints the land.
Mystic echoes softly call,
In the twilight's embrace, we enthrall.

Enigmas drift in ghostly flight,
Veils of secrets hold the night.
The world hushed in reverent glance,
We find peace in night's romance.

Each shadow tells a story old,
Of whispered truths and legends told.
In the twilight's grip, we believe,
In the magic we perceive.

Together we tread on silver ground,
Where silence reigns, and dreams abound.
Beneath the cosmic, swirling dome,
We find in darkness, our true home.

Wardens of the Flickering Chill

Guardians keep a watchful eye,
As winter winds begin to sigh.
In the foggy breath of night,
Flickering flames burn warm and bright.

Through the trees, a whisper flows,
Where the chilling current goes.
Wardens stand with strength and grace,
In the quietude of this place.

Frosted boughs, like jeweled crowns,
Nature's beauty in hushed towns.
Every flicker, a ward against,
The chill that presses, strange and tense.

As shadows gather, weaving tight,
The wardens guard the sacred light.
In unity, they hear a call,
To embrace warmth and not let fall.

As cold deepens, the heart ignites,
In flickering fires, shared delights.
Together we face the bitter night,
With hope and strength, we shine so bright.

Twilight's Empyrean Embrace

In twilight's arms, the heavens sigh,
Where earth and sky in beauty lie.
An empyrean dance unfolds,
As night reveals her secrets bold.

Beneath an arch of starlit grace,
We find the warmth of love's embrace.
The sky ignites in radiant hues,
A canvas brushed with midnight blues.

As day surrenders to the night,
Hope lingers, holding on so tight.
Every star a story spun,
In the silence, dreams are won.

The air is thick with whispered prayers,
As twilight weaves its gentle snares.
Each moment breathes a sacred peace,
While noisy thoughts begin to cease.

In celestial arms, we drift away,
Lost in the magic of the gray.
With eyes closed tightly, hearts unchained,
In twilight's embrace, love is gained.

Resplendent Haze over the Frozen Field

A resplendent haze lays soft and low,
Over fields where cold winds blow.
Whispers of frost dance in the night,
As silence wraps the world in white.

Moonlit footprints trace the ground,
Echoes of stories once profound.
In the soft glow of silver light,
Dreams awaken, taking flight.

Each breath suspended, crisp and clear,
The frozen field invites us near.
With every step, a crystal gleam,
We wander deeper in the dream.

Nature holds its breath with grace,
As moments linger, time's embrace.
In the stillness, hearts unite,
In the world of shadows, pure delight.

Underneath the hazy veil,
We chase the whispers of the pale.
In the frosty air, love reveals,
The beauty found in frozen fields.

The Dance of Light and Chill

In twilight's embrace, the shadows play,
Colors shimmer, then fade away.
Whispers of wind guide the night,
As stars awaken, twinkling bright.

Moonbeams waltz on the frosted ground,
Crickets sing without a sound.
Nature's breath, crisp and clear,
Filling hearts with warmth and cheer.

Branches sway in a gentle sway,
Life's sweet rhythm, night and day.
The chill wraps close, like a shawl,
Inviting dreams with its quiet call.

Frosted leaves, a glistening hue,
Softly reflecting the dreams anew.
In this dance, we twirl and glide,
With every heartbeat, side by side.

As morning breaks, the chill subsides,
Light spills forth where darkness hides.
The dance of light, once more begins,
Warmth returns, as daylight wins.

Sparkling Echoes in the Breeze

Whispers carry on the wind,
Soft and light, where dreams rescind.
Echoes sparkle, bright and clear,
In the distance, songs we hear.

Petals flutter, colors blend,
Nature's beauty, no need to mend.
Underneath the endless sky,
Rippling echoes, soaring high.

Gentle breezes through the trees,
Nature's symphony brings us ease.
Sunlight dances on the ground,
In this moment, peace profound.

Clouds of white drift slowly by,
Painting dreams in the azure sky.
Every sound in harmony,
A tapestry of jubilee.

As the daylight starts to wane,
Twilight's magic, like a chain.
Sparkling echoes, soft and light,
Guide us home through the night.

Silvery Beacons on Frosty Plains

In the stillness, beauty waits,
Silvery beams open the gates.
Frosted meadows, calm and bright,
Glistening stars in the hush of night.

Moonlight bathes the world in white,
Every shadow dances in sight.
The cold air carries a song,
Of silent wonders that dance along.

Across the plains, the whispers flow,
Silver threads where soft winds blow.
Nature's breath, a gentle sigh,
Underneath the vast, open sky.

Moments linger, soft and sweet,
In this frost, our hearts will meet.
Every sparkle, a tale unfolds,
A story of warmth within the cold.

As dawn breaks, the light will shine,
Warming hearts, your hand in mine.
Silvery beacons fade away,
Yet in our hearts, they'll always stay.

Illumination in the Arctic Still

In the Arctic, silence reigns,
Whispers echo through the plains.
Glacial shards of light gleam bright,
A world transformed in purest white.

Beneath the twinkling stars so bold,
Mysteries of ice and cold.
The night holds secrets, still and clear,
In every shadow, love draws near.

Crystalline snows, a blanket spread,
Trail of dreams where hearts are led.
Every glimmer tells a tale,
Of hope and warmth in the frail.

As the night embraces all,
Illumination, we heed the call.
In stillness found, our spirits rise,
Underneath this vast, open sky.

When morning breaks, a new day's song,
In this quiet, we all belong.
Illumination, gentle and true,
Guides our hearts as it ever grew.

Serenity in the Terminated Chill

The air is crisp, a silent sigh,
Clouds drift slowly, time slips by.
Frosted branches, still they stand,
Nature's calm, a gentle hand.

Evening falls; the shadows blend,
Whispers float on winter's wind.
Footsteps crunch on snow's embrace,
In this frozen, peaceful place.

Stars emerge, the night awakes,
Moonlight dances on frozen lakes.
Each breath visible, a soft plume,
Harmony in winter's room.

Solitude holds a tender grace,
Wrapped in nature's cool embrace.
Serenity, a whispered call,
In chilly air, we find it all.

Time stands still, the moment glows,
In the chill, true beauty flows.
A tranquil heart, forever still,
Embraced by winter's serene chill.

Illuminated Whispers in the Snow

Beneath the moon, a soft-lit glow,
Snowflakes twirl in silent flow.
Each one sparkles, a gentle light,
Carving dreams in the blanket white.

Footprints lead to realms unknown,
In this world, we're not alone.
Whispers echo, sweet and low,
Secrets shared beneath the snow.

Stars wink brightly in velvet skies,
While the night softly sighs.
Nature breathes in silent tones,
Creating beauty in frozen bones.

Calm blankets cover weary ground,
In this magic, peace is found.
Illuminated paths we tread,
With every step, new dreams are bred.

In the stillness, hearts unite,
Bonded by the soft, pure light.
Whispers dance like gentle streams,
In snow's embrace, we find our dreams.

Heartbeats in the Glimmering Dusk

The sun dips low, a blaze of gold,
Day's last sigh, a tale retold.
Clouds blush softly, painted hues,
In this moment, hearts muse.

Shadows stretch, as light does fade,
Nature's canvas, finely laid.
Birds return to nests near home,
In this twilight, we gently roam.

The breeze carries a sweet refrain,
Whispers linger, joy unchained.
Each heartbeat echoes with delight,
In the glimmer of fading light.

Stars awaken, one by one,
A tranquil end to day well done.
In dusk's embrace, we find a spark,
Illuminating dreams in the dark.

Together, we share this view,
In silent moments, love feels new.
Heartbeats soft, a rhythmic dance,
In glimmering dusk, we take a chance.

Dissolving Cold in Gleaming Hues

Frost dissolves with morning's kiss,
As sunlight warms, we find our bliss.
Nature sparkles in vibrant cheer,
Colors bloom as winter's clear.

The world awakens; ice retreats,
Gentle whispers, life repeats.
Each flower opens, soft and bright,
Transforming shadows into light.

In this season, hope takes flight,
Chasing away the lingering night.
Every petal tells a tale,
In glowing hues, we shall prevail.

Walking paths lined with renewal,
Hearts are lifted, warm and true.
Spring's embrace, like a melody,
Sings to souls, wild and free.

Dissolving cold, we bid goodbye,
To warmth and joy, we now comply.
In the colors of life anew,
We find our strength in gleaming hues.

Twinkling Hearts Beneath the Frost

In the hush of winter's night,
Stars above begin to glow.
Hearts entwined, a soft delight,
Beneath the frost, love's warmth flows.

Whispers dance through icy air,
Promises wrapped in tender sighs.
Each glance a spark, joy laid bare,
Twinkling hopes beneath the skies.

Frozen branches, silver bright,
Glitter with the morning's cheer.
Embers dance, defying fright,
Hand in hand, we hold what's dear.

Secrets shared beside the light,
Flames that flicker, glimmers bold.
In the silence, hearts unite,
Stories of our love unfold.

Through the chill, we find our way,
Paths illuminated, love's embrace.
In this winter's bright array,
Twinkling hearts forever trace.

Flickering Hopes in the Winter

Snowflakes fall like dreams in flight,
Each one carries whispered cheer.
Hopes that flicker through the night,
Warming souls who gather near.

While the world in white is wrapped,
We ignite our cozy flame.
Holding tight, our fears are trapped,
In this moment, love's the same.

Outside, the cold winds bite and sting,
Yet inside, laughter fills the space.
Flickering hopes begin to sing,
In this winter, we find grace.

Through the chill, our spirit glows,
Like a beacon in the dark.
Strengthened by the love that flows,
Flickering, igniting spark.

Winter nights may be extreme,
But together, we are strong.
In this dance, we find our dream,
Flickering hope, where we belong.

Luminous Shadows Chasing Cold

In twilight's embrace, shadows weave,
Luminous glows push darkness away.
Chasing cold, our hearts believe,
In the warmth of love's gentle play.

Footprints in the winter white,
Mark a path of joy and trust.
Underneath the silver light,
We discover love is a must.

Flickers of warmth within our hands,
Chasing dreams that softly blend.
Through the chill, our spirit stands,
Luminous shadows never end.

In the quiet of the night,
We find solace by the fire.
Luminous hearts, holding tight,
In this moment, we aspire.

Together we will brave the storm,
Finding shelter in each other.
Luminous shadows keeping warm,
Hearts entwined, sister and brother.

Warmth Against the Silent Veil

Against the silent veil of night,
We gather close, a tender heart.
With whispered words, we share our light,
Warmth that shields us from the dark.

Frozen branches, silver lace,
Glisten softly, a fragile dream.
Yet in our hug, we find our place,
Warmth and love, a soothing beam.

Chilling breaths outside our door,
Hold no fear, for we are strong.
In this haven, hearts will soar,
Together here, we both belong.

With every laugh, the night grows bright,
Our spirits blend, a vibrant mix.
Against the cold, we shine our light,
Creating warmth, our joyful fix.

As twilight deepens all around,
We toast to dreams that still remain.
In each other's arms, we're bound,
Warmth against the silent rain.

A Serenade of Light on Winter's Palette

In the hush of twilight's glow,
Snowflakes dance, a gentle show.
Whispers of warmth in the cold air,
A serenade, bright and rare.

Icicles shimmer like crystal stars,
Nature's beauty, no need for jars.
Softly, moonlight paints the ground,
In this silence, peace is found.

Footsteps crunch on frozen paths,
Finding joy in nature's bath.
Each breath a cloud, so soft, so light,
Holding magic in winter's night.

Bringing dreams wrapped in the chill,
Time to ponder, time to fill.
As shadows stretch, the night unfolds,
In this moment, warmth it holds.

Stars above begin to gleam,
Guiding us through the night's dream.
In this stillness, hearts ignite,
Together we bask in the light.

Frost-Kissed Dreams in Silver Radiance

Beneath the moon's soft embrace,
Winter whispers, leaves a trace.
Frost-kissed dreams in shadows play,
Silver radiance, night and day.

Each breath is visible, a dance,
In the stillness, we take a chance.
Warming hearts as darkness creeps,
In this wonder, silence sleeps.

Gentle winds brush the trees,
Carrying laughter on the breeze.
A moment captured, pure and bright,
Frost-kissed magic fills the night.

Stars twinkle in velvet skies,
Wishing upon a dream that flies.
With each glimmer, hope takes flight,
In the cool air, hearts unite.

As dawn approaches, shadows fade,
In this dance, memories made.
Frost-kissed dreams, forever hold,
Tales of winter, softly told.

Solstice Glow in Winter's Quiet Retreat

In the heart of the solstice glow,
Winter whispers, soft and slow.
Quiet retreats in the falling night,
Embraced in warmth, a gentle light.

Crisp air sparkles, stars align,
Echoing dreams, so divine.
Time to ponder, reflect, and see,
The beauty in simplicity.

Fires crackle, shadows dance,
Life unfolds in a blissful trance.
Gather 'round, share your tales,
As the night's soft magic prevails.

Snowflakes twirl in a silent art,
Capturing joy within the heart.
In this stillness, we all find,
A sacred space for the mind.

As winter's veil softly drapes,
Under the moon, the world escapes.
In the embrace, we find our way,
Solstice glow lights up the gray.

Shining Echoes in Night's Embrace

Beneath the stars, the night unfolds,
Shining echoes, stories told.
In the stillness, magic brews,
In winter's arms, the heart renews.

Whispers carried on frosty winds,
A gentle warmth as twilight begins.
Each moment a treasure, soft and bright,
In the embrace of velvet night.

Footsteps lead to paths unknown,
In the dark, their beauty grown.
A quiet journey, souls entwined,
In this glow, our dreams aligned.

Glistening thoughts take to the air,
Wishing for moments we can share.
In the shadows, laughter flows,
With each heartbeat, winter glows.

As dawn approaches with gentle grace,
The world awakens, a new embrace.
Yet in the night, we find our place,
Shining echoes, winter's face.

Twinkling Memories under Glacial Skies

Stars whisper secrets above,
In the stillness of the night.
Memories twinkle like dreams,
Frozen in soft silver light.

Footprints trace paths long walked,
Echoes of laughter resound.
Underneath glacial skies,
Love in silence is found.

Cold winds carry old tales,
Of warmth held in hearts tight.
In the glow of frost-clad trees,
Twinkling memories ignite.

The moon bathes the world in peace,
While shadows dance in the snow.
Each gleam and sparkle a wish,
In the night's tender glow.

As dawn breaks, colors stretch,
Warming the icy terrain.
But the twilight will remind us,
Of memories caught in the chain.

Caress of Resonance in the Frosted Eve

In the hush of twilight's breath,
Whispers weave through the air.
A caress of resonance rings,
In the frost, soft and rare.

Beneath branches layered with snow,
Golden lights flicker and fade.
Echoes of voices long past,
In the evening parade.

Each note a gentle caress,
Dancing through the cold night.
Bound by the warmth of the hearth,
Under stars shining bright.

The world pauses, dreams emerge,
Wrapped in a silver embrace.
In this calm, we remember,
The bonds time cannot erase.

As the moon rises higher,
Stories weave in the frosted eve.
A symphony of connection,
In memories we believe.

Light's Dance on Winter's Breath

Amidst the chill of the night,
Light dances, flickers, and sways.
A ballet on winter's breath,
In the soft hue of the grays.

Crystals shimmer on the ground,
Reflecting a world so bright.
Every flake a story told,
In the calm of the twilight.

Laughter rings through the frost,
As shadows play in delight.
Childhood smiles come alive,
In the wonder of the night.

Branches trace intricate lines,
Against the canvas of stars.
The universe paints with ease,
A masterpiece from afar.

With every breath of the cold,
We find warmth in each other's eyes.
In the glow of winter's light,
Hope forever resides.

Melodies of Warmth Amidst the Chill

In the heart of winter's hold,
Melodies softly unfold.
Warmth spills through the crisp air,
As stories of love are told.

Evenings wrapped in a blanket,
Of laughter, joy, and delight.
While outside the chill lingers,
Inside, hearts feel so light.

Each note a whispering breeze,
Carried on the icy air.
With each song, warmth intensifies,
Binding us in love's glare.

Through frost-painted windows we see,
The world in shimmering white.
But we dance to our rhythms,
In the comfort of this night.

As snowflakes waltz to the ground,
We gather close, hearts entwined.
Melodies wrap around us,
In this season, love defined.

Glowed Secrets in a Cold Landscape

In the hush of winter's hold,
Whispers of warmth still abide,
Beneath the frost, dreams enfold,
Softly in shadows they hide.

Crimson hints on the white ground,
Fleeting moments catch the eye,
In each corner, secrets found,
Where forgotten hopes still lie.

The chill bites, yet hearts ignite,
In the dance of dusk's embrace,
As stars puncture the veil of night,
Revealing tales time cannot erase.

Twinkling fires in icy breath,
Glimmers of stories yet told,
In this landscape, life and death,
Clasp hands with dreams bold.

Each breath a cloud of soul's light,
Yet shadows drape in their guise,
Glowed secrets in the cold night,
Guided by soft, shimmering sighs.

Dappled Light in the Winter's Breath

Morning breaks with gentle grace,
Over slopes crowned in white,
Each crystal flake finds its place,
In the dance of dawn's soft light.

Branches shimmer, delicate show,
Nature's art in silence growing,
Hints of life beneath the snow,
In shadows where warmth is flowing.

Birdsong weaves through frosty air,
Melodies of hope arise,
Love's embrace lingers there,
In the blue of winter skies.

Footprints tell of journeys past,
Echoes of laughter and cheer,
While the moment is held fast,
In the sparkle that draws near.

Dappled light on frozen ground,
Kisses the earth in embrace,
Winter's breath, a lullaby sound,
Whispers the warmth of grace.

Faint Embers in the Whispering Snow

Snowflakes dance on the evening breeze,
Whispering tales of days gone by,
Faint embers glow with gentle ease,
In the hearth where memories lie.

The world outside all dressed in white,
Cocooned in peace, a sacred sight,
Yet deep within, warmth clings tight,
As hearts embrace the soft twilight.

Each flake a story, each drift a song,
Silent echoes of the night,
Where gentle spirits linger long,
In the fading, golden light.

Within the quiet, truth is found,
In the tug of winter's grace,
Faint embers link us, tightly bound,
In this still, enchanted space.

In the hush, a promise made,
That time shall turn the wheel anew,
Faint embers, love's serenade,
In the snow's soft touch, we grew.

Shadows Dancing in Crystalline Air

As twilight drapes the earth in hush,
Spirits twirl with hidden flair,
In the dimming light, we feel the rush,
Of shadows dancing in crystalline air.

Every corner, a flicker of thought,
Figures move with soft delight,
In the embrace of dreams caught,
Where darkness kisses the fading light.

Beneath the stars, the world sighs slow,
Each glimmer a spell we share,
In the cool of night's soft glow,
Whispers twine in the frigid air.

Laughter echoes, then fades away,
As the moon casts its silver stare,
Lost in memories both bright and gray,
In shadows dancing everywhere.

A fleeting moment, a timeless tale,
In the heart of winter's depth,
Where shadows weave and never pale,
In crystalline air, our promise kept.

Warmth Caught in Dappled Light

Sunlight filters through the trees,
Casting shadows bright and free.
Leaves dance softly on the ground,
In this magic, peace is found.

Golden hues of nature's grace,
Wrap the world in warm embrace.
Whispers of the breeze, they play,
Chasing all the chill away.

Hearts awake to summer's call,
In the dappled light, we fall.
Time stands still, while joys ignite,
In warm moments, pure delight.

Every breath a tender sigh,
Underneath the open sky.
Nature's song, a soft respite,
Warmth caught in dappled light.

The Twilit Symphony of Ice and Ember

In twilight's glow, where shadows play,
Ice and ember dance away.
Frosty breath on autumn's flame,
Whispers softly, none to blame.

Crimson skies that fade to grey,
Signals end of the day.
Flickers of warmth in coldest nights,
Melding hues of day and sights.

Harmony of chill and heat,
In every heart, a steady beat.
Nature's pulse in twilight's breath,
Sings of life, and not of death.

The symphony of night unfurls,
Two realms meet, the magic swirls.
Each note a promise softly stems,
The twilit symphony ascends.

Ethereal Glow of Frozen Fantasies

Under starlit skies, dreams unfold,
In frostbit air, a tale is told.
Crystals glimmer, bright and rare,
Whispers float on frosty air.

Each snowflake dances, knows its part,
Painting worlds that touch the heart.
A landscape bright, where shadows gleam,
In frozen fantasies, we dream.

Magic builds in winter's breath,
Forging beauty out of death.
In the stillness, souls ignite,
Ethereal glow, pure and bright.

Each moment holds a secret wish,
In icy realms, we find our bliss.
Lost in thoughts, where we belong,
Frozen fantasies, a cherished song.

Shades of Warmth in the Winter Silence

Softly drapes the winter night,
Blanket holds the world so tight.
Shadows dance near the fireplace,
As time slows down, and thoughts embrace.

Whispers echo, calm and light,
In this hush, hearts feel so right.
The moonlight spills a gentle sheen,
Over dreams that may have been.

Together wrapped in cozy cheer,
In winter's breath, we draw near.
Every glance, a story shared,
In shades of warmth, love declared.

Silent moments, rich and deep,
Carrying promises we keep.
In the winter's quiet grace,
Shades of warmth find their place.

Whispers of Glimmering Chill

In twilight's gentle breath, they sigh,
Soft whispers dance beneath the sky.
The chill bites deep, yet hearts are warm,
As glimmering stars begin to swarm.

A blanket of frost on every tree,
Nature's quiet, a symphony.
Whispers echo in silent night,
Guiding dreams with their muted light.

Fragments of hope in every chill,
Promises wrapped in the quiet thrill.
The world stands still, in peace we find,
A moment frozen, intertwined.

Through shadows flit the memories bright,
Embers that spark in the deepening night.
Each gust carries tales from afar,
In glimmer and chill, we find who we are.

Embered Spirits in Winter's Grasp

In winter's hold, the embers glow,
Spirits dance in the moonlit snow.
Warmth flickers through the frosty air,
Whispers of joy linger everywhere.

Footprints marked in the shimmering white,
Ghostly figures twirl in delight.
A fire crackles, tales come alive,
In winter's grasp, our spirits strive.

Crisp air fills with laughter so clear,
As embers spark and hearts draw near.
The chill enfolds, but warmth remains,
In the dance of spirits, love sustains.

Each gust carries songs of old,
Of fireside stories and memories bold.
In winter's grasp, we find our way,
With embered spirits that light the day.

Silhouettes in the Silver Glow

In silver glow, the night unveils,
Silhouettes cast in moonlit trails.
Figures move with silent grace,
In shadows soft, we find our place.

The world transformed in shades of gray,
Where dreams awaken at close of day.
A dance of light, a fleeting glance,
Silhouettes bound in a gentle trance.

Beneath the stars, we feel the pull,
As time stands still, our hearts are full.
Together we wander through misty nights,
Guided by whispers and silver lights.

With every step, the echoes flow,
Creating paths where futures grow.
In the night's embrace, we come alive,
In silhouettes' stories, together we thrive.

Luminous Shadows of the Night

In the depths where shadows play,
Luminous glimmers light the way.
Stars like jewels in velvet skies,
Whispering secrets, the night replies.

Each shadow dances, smooth and slow,
As moonlight bathes all below.
Luminous threads weave tales anew,
Binding hearts in the shimmering blue.

In twilight's embrace, the world ignites,
With colors rich and pure delights.
Shadows stretch, then softly wane,
Leaving echoes of joy and pain.

The night whispers softly, calls us near,
Luminous visions becoming clear.
In the depths of shadows, we find our soul,
As luminous night takes its toll.

Frosted Flames and Glittering Dreams

In twilight's glow, the chill does bite,
Frosted flames dance, igniting the night.
Whispers of warmth in the silver air,
Glittering dreams, flickering flair.

A crystal world where shadows play,
Embers of hope in cold decay.
Through swirling winds and fading light,
Frosted flames glow, a wondrous sight.

Each breath releases a misty sigh,
Patterns of frost that twinkle, shy.
In the heart of winter, magic brews,
Dreams awaken, and love renews.

With every spark, a story's spun,
Brightening the cold, a race to run.
Together we stand, as silence falls,
Frosted flames under starry thralls.

So let us chase what the night unveils,
In frosted flames, where glitter trails.
A symphony hums, in harmony warm,
Through frost and fire, our spirits swarm.

Radiance Beneath the Ice

Underneath the still, silent sheet,
Radiance hides in the icy seat.
Crystals sparkle, like stars so bright,
Beneath the ice, there's life in sight.

Nature's canvas, a frosty glow,
Whispers of warmth in the cold below.
Frozen rivers, their secrets keep,
Radiance blooms in the winter's sleep.

Glistening paths where shadows tread,
Echoes of light where dreams are bred.
In every flake, a glimmer waits,
Beneath the ice, hope resonates.

Each breath of wind stirs the calm,
Nature's breath, a soothing balm.
From deep within, the light will rise,
Radiance hidden, beneath the skies.

So dance with me in the frosty air,
Together we'll find our fortune rare.
For beneath the ice, our story gleams,
In the heart of winter, lie our dreams.

Glistening Flickers Amongst the Snow

Glistening flickers in the night,
Amongst the snow, a pure delight.
Stars above, like diamonds fall,
Whispers of magic, enchanting call.

Each flake descends, a soft embrace,
Covering earth in silvery lace.
In quiet moments, the world reflects,
Glistening flickers, the heart connects.

In the hush of dusk, a shimmer glows,
Guiding lost souls where beauty flows.
Through snowy fields, our laughter sings,
Glistening joys that winter brings.

With every step, a story laid,
Footprints sparkle, never fade.
Together we weave, through this enchanted,
In glistening flickers, forever granted.

So let us bask in the soft moonlight,
Amongst the snow, our hearts take flight.
For in this moment, dreams unfold,
Glistening flickers, worth more than gold.

Twilight's Warm Embrace

In twilight's grasp, the day does fade,
A warm embrace, in hues displayed.
Golden colors blend into the night,
Soft whispers carry, hearts take flight.

Against the dark, the stars awake,
A tapestry woven, the twilight makes.
With every sigh, the world slows down,
As dusk descends, we wear its crown.

A gentle breeze stirs the leaves,
In twilight's arms, the spirit believes.
Moments linger, as shadows play,
In warm embrace, we find our way.

With every pulse, the magic flows,
Twilight's warmth in every rose.
In the soft glow, our dreams collide,
In twilight's embrace, we find our guide.

So let the night weave its tender thread,
In twilight's glow, all fears we shed.
Together we stand, as stars ignite,
In twilight's warm embrace, all feels right.

Lush Luminescence of Winter Night

In the stillness of the night,
Snowflakes dance, gentle and bright.
Stars twinkle in a velvet sky,
Whispers of winter softly sigh.

Moonlight spills on the frozen ground,
Each shadow a secret, profound.
Branches draped in silver lace,
Nature's beauty, a frozen embrace.

Ice crystals shimmer like diamonds rare,
A tranquil magic fills the air.
Beneath the chill, life's pulse still beats,
In this lush night, the heart retreats.

Through the trees, a soft breeze flows,
Carrying tales that no one knows.
The world wrapped in a blanket white,
A canvas painted by winter's light.

Glistening paths beneath the moon,
Guide dreams that hum a gentle tune.
All is calm, wrapped in the night,
A lullaby of pure delight.

Enchanted Glow in Frostbitten Woods

Deep in the woods where shadows creep,
An enchanted glow stirs from sleep.
Trees stand tall in frosted white,
Guardians of the winter's light.

Frosty breath holds the air so still,
Nature's beauty, a quiet thrill.
Crystalline branches softly gleam,
Living within a frozen dream.

Footfalls quiet on the cold ground,
A whispered hush, a sacred sound.
Gazed skies weave tales of the night,
In shimmering threads of purest light.

Glow of moonbeams through leaves unseen,
Creates a magic felt, serene.
In this realm where silence speaks,
The heart, in wonder, gently peaked.

Stars twinkle like secrets shared,
In the tranquility, souls are bared.
Embraced by night, dreams take flight,
Awash in the enchanted light.

Veils of Light in a Frozen Realm

Beneath the veil of a frosty dawn,
A realm of wonder magically drawn.
Glistening snow on the forest floor,
Whispers of light gently implore.

The air is crisp with a lure divine,
A world cloaked in sparkling design.
Veils of light weave through the trees,
Caressing the earth with a silent breeze.

Colorless hues start to glow,
Illuminating paths where few dare go.
In this frozen land, dreams emerge,
From the depths of winter, life does surge.

Fragrant pine hangs heavy, near,
Echoes of laughter, faint yet clear.
Where frost meets the sun, new stories unfold,
In the frozen arms of winter's hold.

The tapestry glows with celestial light,
Guiding hearts through the cold of night.
A frozen treasure, bartered and kept,
In veils of light, the world has wept.

Sparked Dreams at the Edge of Night

As twilight wraps the day in embrace,
Sparked dreams float in a tranquil space.
Far horizons kissed by the glow,
Of stars that whisper secrets slow.

The edge of night unveils the sky,
Where wishes flutter, soar and fly.
In shadows cast by the fading light,
Hope glimmers, bold and bright.

Winter's breath carries tales untold,
Of adventures brave and dreams of old.
Through icy fingers, wishes gleam,
On the brink of a waking dream.

A canvas blank, awaits the brush,
In twilight's hush, a gentle rush.
Hearts aglow with unspoken lore,
As night unfolds, they seek for more.

Stars wink down like playful wraiths,
Calling forth those hidden faiths.
In the silence, visions take flight,
Sparked dreams embrace the edge of night.

Soft Flickers on Crystal Flesh

In the twilight's embrace, soft glimmers play,
Whispers of light dance, gently they sway.
Fragile reflections on the skin's sheen,
A world caught in shimmer, serene and unseen.

Glistening secrets in the night's cool breath,
Moments suspended between life and death.
A touch of magic in the silent night,
Soft flickers glow, casting shadows bright.

Dew-kissed petals glow under the moon,
Nature's soft canvas, a fleeting tune.
Each shimmer a promise of dreams yet to chase,
In this radiant realm, we find our place.

Echoes of laughter in the shimmering dew,
Captured emotions of me and you.
The night's gentle arms cradle our grace,
Wrapped in soft flickers, time slows its pace.

Crystals of starlight adorn the ground,
In this paradise, tranquility found.
As dawn approaches, the magic will fade,
But in our hearts, the memories stayed.

Ember's Breath in the Frosty Breeze

The fire's warmth glows in the winter's chill,
A crackling heartbeat, a warmth to fulfill.
Embers whisper secrets to the frozen air,
As frost bites tenderly, unaware of despair.

Dancing flames twirl in a swirling mist,
Each flicker carries a forgotten twist.
Voices of fire sing sweet lullabies,
Ember's breath lingers as the cold wind tries.

In twilight's fold, warmth softly confides,
Creating a haven where comfort abides.
The frost may wander, relentless and bold,
But embers embrace with a glow wrapped in gold.

As shadows stretch long beneath the pale moon,
The firelight flickers, a composed tune.
In the frosty breeze, hear the heartbeat's call,
Ember's sweet breath breaks the night's frozen thrall.

With each passing hour, the darkness will fade,
But ember's sweet warmth in our souls won't degrade.
We carry that fire till the end of our days,
In the frost, find comfort, embrace life's warm rays.

Secrets of the Glowing Ember

In the heart of the night, a treasure does gleam,
Secrets of embers whisper, like a dream.
Hidden in shadows, stories unfold,
Tales etched in silence, precious and bold.

Each flicker reveals a moment in time,
Echoes of laughter in a life so sublime.
The glowing ember shares its bright lore,
Reminders of warmth that we all can explore.

In its soft pulsing, the universe breathes,
Crafting a tapestry from passion it weaves.
The warmth in the dark is a promise unspoken,
Ember's warm glow, never to be broken.

Listen closely; the flames have a tale,
Of love's gentle hardship and dreams that prevail.
Cocooned in its light, the world stands still,
Secrets of embers, are whispers that thrill.

As dawn draws near and shadows retreat,
Embers fade lightly, with a pain bittersweet.
Yet in every heart, their stories remain,
The glowing ember's secrets, forever sustain.

Ice-Kissed Flames of Solitude

In the still of the night, where silence reigns,
Ice-kissed flames flicker, breaking the chains.
Loneliness dances, swirling in space,
Yet warmth ignites in the cold's tight embrace.

The fire burns quietly, a solitary glow,
Melting the frost in the heart's tender throe.
Embers reflect on the icy terrain,
As solitude wraps like a comforting chain.

Each spark tells a story, alone yet alive,
In the depths of the night, the spirit will thrive.
From ashes of sorrow, new warmth will arise,
Ice-kissed flames flicker under darkened skies.

The world may grow distant, but light remains near,
A beacon of hope when the path isn't clear.
Solitude whispers in the hushed lullaby,
Ice-kissed flames glimmer, as time drifts by.

As morning approaches, and shadows retreat,
The icy chill softens, night bows in defeat.
Yet the warmth of the flame, in stillness will stay,
In the heart of solitude, she softly will play.

Reflections in the Winter's Whisper

In the quiet woods, shadows dance,
Snowflakes twirl in the fleeting glance.
Whispers echo through the trees,
Carrying secrets on the chilling breeze.

Pine branches arch with a snowy crown,
Softly bending, never to frown.
Footprints lead to the frozen stream,
Where winter weaves its silver dream.

Beneath a blanket of gentle white,
The world rests peacefully in twilight.
Each breath, a fog against the chill,
Nature's heart beats, steady and still.

Reflections cast on ice-bound lakes,
Memories linger, the spirit awakes.
As the sun dips low, hues intertwine,
In winter's embrace, everything aligns.

A final hush before the dark,
Stars emerge with a twinkling spark.
In this serene, magical hour,
The night blooms softly, a frosted flower.

Frosty Gleams of Distant Worlds

Stars linger on the winter's breath,
Winking softly, defying death.
Their glimmers shimmer like distant dreams,
Floating softly on moonlit beams.

Wrapped in blankets of shimmering white,
Nature sleeps, cloaked in night.
Each sparkle whispers tales untold,
Of timeless wonders, fierce and bold.

The heavens mirror the snow-clad ground,
In this stillness, a beauty profound.
Whispers from galaxies far and near,
Echo softly, clear and dear.

Frosty petals on the windowpanes,
Nature's art where silence reigns.
Every breath is a tender sigh,
As the universe winks from the sky.

In the frosty gleams, secrets blend,
Each night's promise, a hopeful mend.
We wander lost in this celestial glow,
Finding solace in the chill and snow.

Ethereal Light in Frigid Air

A pale sun rises, shy and slow,
Casting shadows on the frozen glow.
Light dances lightly, a gentle sway,
Painting frost with shades of gray.

Trees transformed, a crystal sight,
Branches adorned, pure and bright.
In this realm where silence sings,
The magic of winter unfurls its wings.

Icy breath weaves through the dawn,
Threads of silver on the lawn.
Each step taken, a soft crunch near,
In the chill, the world feels clear.

Beneath the frost, life holds tight,
Behind the cold, there lies pure light.
In every flake that drifts and sways,
Lives a beauty that forever stays.

As the day wanes, colors ignite,
A canvas rich in warm twilight.
In the frigid air, hope does bloom,
Ethereal light dispels the gloom.

Warmth Against Winter's Breath

A crackling fire, soft and bright,
Filling spaces with golden light.
In its glow, stories unfold,
Of summers past and dreams retold.

Outside, the world wears winter's veil,
While inside, love weaves its tale.
Hot cocoa steaming in the cup,
Hearts find refuge, spirits lift up.

Windows framed with frost and ice,
Desire dances, warm and nice.
Here, within these cherished walls,
Laughter echoes, the winter calls.

Amidst the cold, we gather near,
In every smile, a warmth sincere.
Through frosty nights and icy dawns,
Our bonds grow tighter, winter's fawns.

As the season shifts, we hold our ground,
In every heartbeat, love is found.
Against winter's breath, we stand as one,
While the cold whispers, we've just begun.

Luminance in the Icy Air

Stars twinkle in the frozen night,
Whispers of dreams take flight.
Moonlight dances on the snow,
Guiding hearts wherever they go.

Frosty breath in the stillness speaks,
Nature rests, yet beauty peaks.
Crystals sparkle, a wondrous sight,
In the icy air, pure delight.

Glistening trees stand tall and proud,
Cloaked in silence, wrapped in a shroud.
Each branch adorned, a masterpiece,
In winter's clutch, a moment of peace.

A hush falls softly, enveloping all,
In the frosty embrace, we stand small.
With each heartbeat echoing clear,
Luminance glows in the icy air.

Under the calm, a world renews,
In every flake, a thousand hues.
Nature's canvas, vast and grand,
In this beauty, we take our stand.

Glistening Reflections at Dusk

As the sun dips low and shadows fall,
The sky ignites, a brilliant sprawl.
Brushing light with hues of gold,
Whispers of evening stories unfold.

Rippling waters catch the glow,
Mirrored dreams in ebb and flow.
Azure skies turn amber bright,
In glistening moments, we find our light.

Gentle breezes caress the air,
Casting spells everywhere.
Nature stitches day into night,
With every stitch, a tranquil sight.

A canvas painted with fervent care,
Reflections swirl, a dance so rare.
Timeless echoes of whispered grace,
In the twilight's warm embrace.

Stars begin to peek and shine,
A celestial dance, perfectly fine.
With every glow, a promise made,
In glistening reflections, dreams will wade.

Serenity in Silhouette

Silhouettes dance against the night,
Figures moving, soft and light.
Fingers trace the edge of dreams,
In shadows deep, nothing's as it seems.

A quiet breath beneath the moon,
The world slows down, a gentle tune.
Brushstrokes of dark on a glowing sky,
In the silence, our spirits fly.

Beneath the stars, we find our peace,
In stillness, we let worries cease.
Waves of calm on a tender breeze,
Serenity whispers through the trees.

Every contour holds a story,
In the quiet, find your glory.
A tapestry woven, soft and bold,
In the silhouette, our lives unfold.

Hearts entwined in the dusk's embrace,
Every moment, time leaves a trace.
In the beauty of the starry night,
Serenity blooms in soft twilight.

The Warmth of a Flickering Heart

In the gentle glow of a candle's light,
Embers dance in the still of night.
Flickers whisper ancient tales,
Of love enduring, where hope prevails.

A heartbeat echoes, steady and true,
Each pulse reminds me of you.
In shadows cast by the fire's kiss,
I find warmth, I find bliss.

The world outside fades to a sigh,
Within this moment, we simply fly.
Wrapped in the comfort of your gaze,
Time stands still in this soft haze.

A promise held in flickering flame,
With every spark, love calls your name.
In the warmth of night, our souls unite,
Together we're perfect, together we're right.

Let the world turn, let seasons change,
In our hearts, nothing feels strange.
For in the quiet, I always see,
The warmth of your flickering heart with me.

Soft Glows on Frozen Ground

In the silence of winter's night,
Soft glows whisper, pure and bright.
Moonlight dances on the snow,
Painting dreams where shadows flow.

Frosty breath of trees so tall,
Wrapped in crystal, nature's thrall.
Stars above like diamonds gleam,
Binding the world in a silver dream.

Each flake that falls is a gentle muse,
Crafting tales in frost-kissed hues.
The earth holds secrets in its grasp,
As frozen whispers breathe and clasp.

Quiet moments, hearts will mend,
In this stillness, sorrows end.
Soft glows on the frozen ground,
In winter's embrace, peace is found.

So wander forth with open eyes,
Beneath the hush of starlit skies.
For in the cold, warmth can thrive,
In the soft glows, we come alive.

The Hearth's Gentle Caress

The hearth, alive with crackling cheer,
Beckons loved ones gathered near.
Flames dance and sway, a warm embrace,
Kindling smiles on every face.

Golden light spills across the floor,
Stories shared forevermore.
In this circle, hearts ignite,
The world's woes fade from sight.

Whispers of kindness fill the air,
In the warmth, we shed our care.
The gentle caress of flames so bright,
Chasing away the depths of night.

As shadows play upon the walls,
The hearth's glow, a melody calls.
Embers speak of dreams and quests,
In gentle heat, the spirit rests.

Together in this sacred space,
We forge bonds that time can't erase.
In the hearth's embrace, we find our place,
Wrapped in love, we hold our grace.

Shattered Stars on Icy Serpents

On the frozen lake's dark expanse,
Shattered stars in a wild dance.
Their brilliance pierces the cold night,
Guiding lost wanderers with light.

Icy serpents twist and weave,
Guarding secrets few perceive.
Beneath the surface, shadows play,
As flickering dreams begin to sway.

Whispers of magic fill the air,
In the depths, hidden treasures stare.
Each glimmer tells a tale untold,
Of warmth and wonder in the cold.

Bathed in moon's soft, silvery glow,
Shattered stars above us flow.
In the chill, our hearts ignite,
Finding solace in the night.

So step with care on precious ice,
Where dreams and dangers intertwine nice.
Shattered stars guide the way,
In icy embrace, let spirits sway.

Glowing Hearts Amidst the Cold

In the depth of winter's freeze,
Glowing hearts will find their ease.
Through the chill, we rise and stand,
Bound together, hand in hand.

Frosty breath paints the night,
Stars above, a guiding light.
In this frost-kissed world, we grow,
With love that flickers, warm and slow.

Each heartbeat, a gentle flame,
In the cold, we fan the same.
Through the darkness, warmth will spread,
In glowing hearts, hope is fed.

Though snow may blanket all around,
Our spirits soar, unbound, profound.
Nature whispers in the hush,
As glowing hearts feel the rush.

So let the frost come and fall,
For love's light conquers all.
Amidst the cold, we shine so bright,
Glowing hearts, a beacon of light.

The Fusion of Flame and Frost

In twilight's dance, the colors blend,
Where fire meets the chill, they mend.
A flicker warms the icy air,
A bright embrace, a whispered dare.

The embers spark in frosted night,
While icy shards reflect the light.
Together they create a vow,
A moment held, a timeless now.

The fusion ripples through the ground,
Creating harmony profound.
Each flame a whisper, each frost a sigh,
Together beneath the vast, dark sky.

Through fire's heart and frost's intent,
A beauty born, a love unbent.
In every breath, in every gleam,
They weave together, a shared dream.

In this embrace, the world ignites,
With passion born in tranquil nights.
A dance eternal, ever bright,
This fusion glows, igniting light.

Winter's Glow Whispers of Light

Softly falling on the ground,
A delicate, enchanting sound.
The snowflakes glisten, pure and bright,
Winter's glow whispers of light.

A gentle breeze through branches sways,
In silver tones, the twilight plays.
With every step, the earth feels right,
As winter's glow whispers of light.

The stars above begin to blink,
In vivid hues, they start to think.
With every heartbeat, hope ignites,
In winter's glow, whispers of light.

The world adorned in glistening white,
A canvas blank, so pure, so bright.
Each shadow cast, a tale in sight,
Of winter's glow, whispers of light.

Through frosty nights the stories flow,
Of dreams long past, and futures slow.
In nature's calm, all feels so right,
As winter's glow whispers of light.

Flickering Solitude amid Crystalline Silence

In the hush of night, time slows,
A flicker here, just one that glows.
Amongst the stars, silent and bright,
A solitude wrapped in pure light.

The crystals form a frozen dream,
Reflecting all in silver gleam.
Each quiet moment lingers near,
In flickering solitude, sincere.

Emotions swirl like snowflakes drift,
In icy air, a subtle gift.
The world outside feels far away,
In this stillness, hearts convey.

The flicker dances, soft and true,
Illuminating thoughts anew.
In crystalline silence, whispers play,
Flickering solitude lights the way.

With every breath, the cosmos sighs,
In winter's grasp, the heart relies.
Within this peace, the soul takes flight,
In flickering solitude and light.

Cold Embrace of the Illuminated Night

The stars awake, a distant sight,
In cold embrace of illuminated night.
Whispers travel on the breeze,
A tender touch that chills and frees.

The moonlit path invites the stray,
To wander forth, where shadows play.
In every corner, secrets hide,
In this embrace, the dreams abide.

The frost adorns the sleeping trees,
With silver lace in tranquil freeze.
Each breath a cloud, a fleeting thought,
In cold embrace, the warmth is sought.

The night unfolds with tales untold,
In quiet grace, the heart feels bold.
Underneath the heaven's light,
We find our way, our guiding sight.

In unity, the world refrains,
From winter's grasp to hopeful gains.
With every star that shines so bright,
We cherish cold, illuminated night.

Nocturnal Sparks in the Snowfield

Stars flicker in the night,
A blanket of white below,
Footprints left by soft steps,
Whispers carried by the snow.

Silent trees stand tall and bright,
Embers caught in frozen air,
Dreams dance amidst the dark,
With a magic that feels rare.

Moonlight spills on crystal ground,
Shadows play in soft embrace,
In the stillness, hearts are found,
Time slows down in this space.

Frosty breath, a gentle sight,
Starlit skies, a soothing balm,
Sparkling doubts take flight,
Nature's touch, a tender calm.

Night embraces every glow,
Nocturnal sparks, a warm delight,
In the silence, let it flow,
Wonders born from purest night.

Hidden Fires Beneath the Surface

Beneath the ice, warmth lingers,
Fires glow in secret folds,
Silent passion, bright fingers,
Stories whispered, yet untold.

In the depths, where shadows creep,
Burning embers wait to rise,
Awakened from their frozen sleep,
Offering heat beneath the skies.

Cracks appear, the surface breaks,
With each moment, warmth ignites,
Life reclaims what winter takes,
Hidden fires, newfound lights.

Cinders glow in chilly air,
Soft reminders of the past,
Underneath the frosty layer,
Fires burn, forever last.

Passions simmer, never fade,
Underneath the surface lies,
A world of dreams, all handmade,
Where the heart's true fire thrives.

Whispers of Warmth in a Frozen Veil

Amid the frost, a tender call,
Whispers dance on winter's breath,
Gentle tones that softly fall,
Promises held within the depth.

Veils of snow wrap earth in sleep,
Yet warmth lingers, shall not hide,
In the quiet, secrets seep,
Embers glow where dreams abide.

Soft embraces in the chill,
Melodies of fate align,
Cocooned hearts with hopes to fill,
Tender whispers intertwine.

Under layers, love persists,
In the frost, a fire blooms,
Each caress a moment missed,
Life's sweet warmth in winter's glooms.

Frozen world, so bold and bright,
Yet within, a gentle flame,
In the shadows, find your light,
Whispers speak your truest name.

Glistening Wishes on the Frosty Path

Footprints mark a icy trail,
Snowflakes dance, a silver glow,
Wishes caught in frosty air,
Voices murmur soft and low.

Dreams reflect in glistening white,
Each star a wish in the night,
Frosty breath and hearts alight,
Guided by the moon's soft sight.

Every step, a tale unfolds,
Paths entwined in crisp delight,
Glistening hopes, like scattered gold,
Lead us on through starry night.

In the stillness, magic stirs,
Winter's hush, a quiet song,
Find the warmth where love occurs,
In this realm, we all belong.

With each wish, the world awakes,
Underneath the velvet sky,
In frost's grip, our spirit shakes,
Creating dreams that dare to fly.

Whispers in the Winter Glow

The snowflakes fall, soft and slow,
As twilight casts a gentle show.
In whispered hush, the cold winds blow,
Nature sings in winter's glow.

Branches creak under their weight,
While silence drapes the night so late.
In the stillness, dreams await,
In cozy nooks, we contemplate.

A fire crackles, warmth surrounds,
With each flicker, magic sounds.
In every corner, joy abounds,
As love and laughter wrap the grounds.

The stars emerge, a sparkling sea,
In this moment, just you and me.
With every glance, our hearts agree,
In winter's grasp, we are set free.

So let the world outside be cold,
In our embrace, we find our gold.
Whispers of dreams, now retold,
In winter's beauty, love unfolds.

Shadows Dance in the Silvery Night

Underneath the silver moon,
Whispers float in sweet soft tune.
Shadows dance, a lively swoon,
In the heart of night, we croon.

A breeze arrives with secrets bare,
Tickling leaves, teasing air.
Every corner, moments shared,
In the magic, none compare.

Stars above like diamonds bright,
Guide our steps, a gentle light.
In this calm, we lose the fight,
To the shadows, pure delight.

Echoes of laughter, soft and clear,
In the stillness, love draws near.
Within these walls, there's naught to fear,
In shadow's dance, we persevere.

As dawn approaches, colors bloom,
Yet still, within this silent room.
We'll hold tight to night's perfume,
And cherish shadows that consume.

Embrace of the Amber Flame

In the hearth, the embers glow,
Flickering tales of long ago.
With every crackle, feelings flow,
The warmth enchants, a soft tableau.

Golden light on faces bright,
In the dim, we find our sight.
Together, our hearts take flight,
In the amber flame, pure delight.

Stories whispered, hopes ignite,
In this embrace, all feels right.
With every gaze, we share the night,
The world fades, lost from our sight.

Time drips slow, like honey's stream,
Wrapped in warmth, we cling to dream.
In the fire's glow, love will gleam,
An eternal dance, a perfect theme.

So let the flames call out our names,
With every flicker, passion claims.
In this space where nothing's lame,
We bask forever in love's flames.

Frosted Dreams Under Dim Stars

Beneath a quilt of sparkling frost,
In whispers soft, we find what's lost.
Time slows down, love's gentle cost,
Together here, we're never tossed.

The night unfolds with silver light,
Dreams entwined in starry flight.
In the quiet, hearts unite,
Underneath the cosmic sight.

Drawn closer by the chilling air,
With frosted breath, we make a pair.
Every moment, magic rare,
In the night, with memories share.

The world outside, a sleeping place,
In our hearts, we find a space.
Under stars, we trace each face,
In frozen dreams, our love's embrace.

So let the night be calm and deep,
In this moment, secrets keep.
For in our dreams, we softly leap,
In frosted whispers, love's pure sweep.

Memoirs of Light in Frigid Air

Whispers of dawn in the icy haze,
Memories linger, in twilight's gaze.
Fragments of warmth in the biting chill,
Echoes of laughter, the heart feels still.

Stars softly twinkle, a distant glow,
Frosted whispers where the cold winds blow.
Breath of the night, so crisp and clear,
Guiding the soul, that feels it near.

Dreams drift like snowflakes, delicate flight,
In a canvas of silver, the darkness bites.
Yet with each shimmer, a promise unfolds,
Of stories retold, in the freeze it holds.

Hands reach for warmth, where shadows play,
In the embrace of the cold, we find our way.
Moments of silence, wrapped in the light,
Illuminate paths in the depth of night.

Through the frigid air, the heart will sing,
Of memories cherished, the joy they bring.
In icy realms, where solitude reigns,
Hope flickers gently, as love sustains.

Frost Over the Flickering Soul

In shadows of winter, a flame half-glows,
Veiled in the frost, where the cold wind blows.
A whisper of dreams, in frozen breath,
The flickering heart wrestles with death.

Brittle leaves rustle, in stillness they weep,
Under the weight of the secrets we keep.
Flames dance in silence, longing for light,
Yearning for warmth in the heart of the night.

Glimmers of hope, like stars in the dark,
Guide weary travelers with each tiny spark.
Chilled by the night, yet longing for warmth,
The soul seeks comfort, a safe spot to form.

In the frost's embrace, we struggle and strive,
Through whispers of sorrow, we still survive.
With each frozen breath, we declare our will,
To rise from the ashes, and conquer the chill.

So let the frost over our spirits lay,
For soon shall the dawning reveal a new day.
And in that warmth, we shall find our role,
A dance of resilience, the flickering soul.

Stillness Beneath the Soft Radiance

Quietude rests in the morning's embrace,
A blanket of snow, a delicate lace.
Beneath its stillness, a heartbeat remains,
In the hush of the world, where calmness reigns.

Gentle the light that breaks through the night,
Kissing the day with a tender delight.
A chorus of silence, and nature's pure art,
In this soft radiance, we mend the heart.

Branches adorned with their crystalline crowns,
Whisper of peace beneath winter's frowns.
For in the soft glow, the spirit finds grace,
In the fleeting moments, we find our space.

As shadows retreat in the warmth of the morn,
The stillness awakens, a new light is born.
In the fragile beauty of this frozen sigh,
We dance with the echoes that never say die.

So cherish each heartbeat, embrace the serene,
For within the stillness, we find what has been.
A journey of solace, a pathway to whole,
Under the soft radiance, we revive the soul.

Emotions Burn Bright in the Cold

In the frost-kissed air, fires flicker and spark,
Emotions awaken in the silence so stark.
Hearts wrapped in warmth, though the chill lingers near,
Bright embers of love drown out all the fear.

Each glance, a flame that dances and sways,
Igniting the passion in the cold's harsh gaze.
For warmth isn't found in mere heat of the day,
But in the fierce glow when the shadows betray.

Underneath layers where the cold dare to creep,
Lives a bright flame that the heart longs to keep.
Through the icy struggles and battles we face,
The fire of emotions, a warm, sacred place.

So let not the winter dim the colors we feel,
For in every heartbeat, there lies a great zeal.
Flames that burn bright beneath icy repose,
Conjure up courage, as the heart bravely glows.

In the stillness of night, when the world feels so bold,
Remember the warmth in your spirit to hold.
As emotions burn bright in the depth of the fold,
Life's symphony echoes, turning silver to gold.

Silvered Light on Frosted Glass

In dawn's embrace, a soft glow speaks,
Whispers of warmth caress the cold peaks.
Silvered light in delicate dance,
Framed by frost, a fleeting chance.

Each breath of morning, a crystalline show,
Nature's mirror reflects the glow.
Patterns weave in a frosted dream,
Unraveling mysteries in silent stream.

Awakening hearts with a gentle start,
Silvered shards artfully part.
Glimmers of hope, a tranquil sight,
Embracing winter's enchanting light.

As shadows shift with the day's advance,
Every crystal spark holds a secret glance.
In stillness wrapped, the world holds its breath,
Silvered light whispers tales of depth.

Glow of Resilience Against the Frost

Amidst the chill, a warmth remains,
Glints of hope through winter's chains.
Each ember bright, a story told,
Of hearts that shine when the world feels cold.

Under snowy blankets, tough roots dig deep,
In the frozen embrace, dreams still leap.
Nature's will, in colors bold,
Resilience shines as the frost enfolds.

The quiet strength of each fragile stem,
Fighting back where the shadows hem.
Against the frost, their spirits soar,
Glow of resilience, forevermore.

In the darkest nights, they bravely stand,
A flicker of light in a frozen land.
Winter's harsh grip may stifle the scene,
Yet life's warm glow speaks strong and keen.

Dances of Light on Winter's Edge

At twilight's hour, the world glimmers,
Dances of light where frost shimmers.
A ballet of colors, crisp and bright,
Horizon embraces the enchanting night.

Each twirl of snowflakes, a soft embrace,
Swirling patterns in a tranquil space.
Lights flicker softly, a gentle cue,
Winter's edge breathes in hues of blue.

Footsteps crunching on paths of white,
Bathed in glows, hearts feel light.
Nature's stage, where magic unfolds,
Dances of light, a wonder retold.

As starlight twinkles above the trees,
A symphony echoes in the winter breeze.
Holding memories close, shadows take flight,
In the dances of light on winter's night.

Charmed Radiance of a Winter's Night

Under a canopy of dark, vast skies,
Charmed radiance glows, as silence sighs.
Snowflakes shimmer in lunar beams,
Painting the world with luminous dreams.

Every breath, a cloud of mist,
A serene beauty that can't be missed.
Stars whisper secrets to the frosty air,
Winter's magic, enchanting and rare.

In the stillness, hearts entwine,
Bathed in the glow, where spirits shine.
The night unfolds its tranquil grace,
Charmed radiance, a warm embrace.

Flakes as soft as a lover's touch,
Embracing the world, meaning so much.
In midnight's hold, dreams take their flight,
Charmed radiance warms the winter's night.

Dreams Woven in Glowing Threads

In twilight's grasp, visions arise,
Threads of hope weave through the skies.
Upon the loom, desires dance,
In whispered dreams, we find our chance.

Stars spin tales, softly they glow,
Guiding hearts where wishes flow.
Each shimmering strand, a story told,
In the fabric of night, our dreams unfold.

Colors blend in the midnight hue,
A tapestry bright, both bold and true.
With each heartbeat, the weaves get tight,
Embracing the wonders of starlit night.

Awake we stand, as dawn draws near,
Carrying dreams that we hold dear.
With glowing threads, we'll shape our fate,
In the light of day, we celebrate.

So let us wear this crafted gown,
Stitched with love, never let it drown.
In dreams woven with the night's sweet breath,
We'll find our purpose, defying death.

Heat Found in the Chilly Air

Beneath a blanket of frosty white,
Whispers of warmth ignite the night.
In stillness deep, a spark ignites,
Embers glow in the chilly bites.

Breath of winter, crisp and clear,
Yet passion's fire draws us near.
Hands entwined against the deep cold,
In our embrace, the warmth unfolds.

Snowflakes dance in their frosty flight,
Yet hearts beat loud, filling the night.
Through biting winds and frozen leaves,
We find the heat that never leaves.

In the chilled air, laughter rings,
Softly wrapped in the joy it brings.
With every heartbeat, the world feels light,
Finding warmth in the starry night.

So let the frost fall all around,
In vibrant love, our dreams are found.
Together we'll weather the winter's chill,
With heat ablaze, and hearts to fill.

Illuminated Shadows in a Snowy World

In a still world blanketed white,
Shadows flicker, soft and light.
Moonbeams dance on the glistening ground,
In this silence, magic is found.

Each step leaves a trace in the snow,
Carving paths where dreams might go.
Illuminated whispers call the night,
Bringing wonder, a gentle sight.

Trees stand tall, cloaked in frost,
Frozen beauty that cannot be lost.
In the hush, secrets softly lay,
Illuminated shadows lead the way.

Cold breath of night wraps around,
Yet warmth of wonder can be found.
As shadows shimmer, we are drawn,
To a world alive, where dreams are spawned.

In this snowy realm, hearts awake,
Illuminated paths, we dare to take.
Through snowy nights, with stars so bright,
Shadows guide us to morning light.

Echoes of Light in the Frosty Stillness

In the quiet, where echoes reside,
Light dances softly, a fleeting guide.
Frosty stillness, a blanket wide,
In this moment, our souls confide.

Glimmers shine in the pale moon's glow,
Whispering secrets, soft and low.
Every ray, a touch from above,
Filling the silence with whispers of love.

Footsteps trace through the icy night,
Chasing shadows that bathe in light.
Each echo sings of what once was,
In the stillness, our hearts pause.

Beneath the stars, hopes come alive,
In frost's embrace, we learn to thrive.
Light's echo carries, gentle yet clear,
In the stillness, we draw near.

So let us breathe in the night so cold,
With echoes of warmth that never grow old.
In frost and brilliance, we will find,
The echoes of light that bind us, entwined.

Dreams Rise with the Gentle Blaze

In the quiet night they gleam,
A flicker born from whispers' seam.
Soft embers dance to a sweet soft tune,
As hopes arise beneath the moon.

They float like feathers, light and free,
Carried forth by a tender plea.
In every spark, a wish takes flight,
Dreams rise slowly, igniting the night.

With every crackle, secrets unfold,
Stories of yearning, connected yet bold.
The warmth they share calms every fear,
In gentle blaze, dreams persevere.

Embers glow with a golden glow,
Binding hearts that should not let go.
Together they flicker, together they rise,
Illuminating the darkening skies.

So tend the flame, keep it alive,
In the gentle blaze, the dreams will thrive.
In every heart, a flicker remains,
In this sacred warmth, love sustains.

Hallowed Ground in Frigid Light

Amidst the frost, whispers abound,
In the silence, hallowed ground.
Each snowflake falls, a story so fine,
A moment captured, pure and divine.

Fingers entwined in winter's embrace,
Traces of warmth in a cold, lonely space.
With every breath, the stillness sighs,
As love's warmth against the frost tries.

Glistening leaves, a crystal display,
Each shimmering shard leads our way.
In frigid light where spirits sing,
The heart finds peace, and hope takes wing.

Here in the still, where time feels paused,
The world is wrapped in a velvet cause.
In the cold, we gather, steadfast and bright,
Hallowed ground in the frigid light.

Clarity blooms with silent delight,
In this frozen realm, spirits ignite.
Together we stand, hand in hand tight,
Bound by the magic of the night.

Glows of Love in a Crystal Maze

In corridors of ice where shadows play,
Glows of love light our tangled way.
Every turn, a path unknown,
Yet warmth and laughter make it our own.

Through frosted mirrors, reflections gleam,
Carved in time, life's fleeting dream.
In dazzling light, our spirits soar,
In the maze of heart, we seek for more.

Twinkling wonders around each bend,
In crystal whispers, hopes transcend.
Each heartbeat echoes, a soft refrain,
Amongst the glows, we break each chain.

Hand in hand through this maze we roam,
In each corner, we find our home.
With every step, our love defies,
In this labyrinth, our spirits rise.

So let us wander, lost in delight,
Through the glows of love, dispelling the night.
In every glimmer, a promise we make,
In this crystal maze, together we wake.

Flickering Truths Beneath the Ice

Beneath the surface, whispers dwell,
Flickering truths only time can tell.
In layers thick, dark secrets hide,
Yet warmth and light cannot be denied.

Through cracks of hope, the daylight seeps,
In frozen depths, a heart still beats.
Each truth revealed warms the chill,
Breaking the silence, bending our will.

With every flicker, shadows retreat,
As light dances, fear meets defeat.
In the thawing ground, life finds its way,
Flickering truths lead us through the fray.

In the depths where the coldness bites,
We search for warmth in the darkest nights.
Each icy facade starts to melt,
In flickering truths, our hearts are felt.

So gather close, share what we hide,
In flickering truths, let love be our guide.
Transform the depths where silence dared,
In this radiant glow, together we've shared.